CENGAGE Learning

Novels for Students, Volume 7

Staff

Series Editor: Deborah A. Stanley.

Contributing Editors: Sara L. Constantakis, Catherine L. Goldstein, Motoko Fujishiro Huthwaite, Arlene M. Johnson, Erin White.

Editorial Technical Specialist: Karen Uchic.

Managing Editor: Joyce Nakamura.

Research: Victoria B. Cariappa, *Research Team Manager*. Andy Malonis, *Research Specialist*. Tamara C. Nott, Tracie A. Richardson, and Cheryl L. Warnock, *Research Associates*. Jeffrey Daniels, *Research Assistant*.

Permissions: Susan M. Trosky, *Permissions Manager*. Maria L. Franklin, *Permissions Specialist*. Sarah Chesney, *Permissions Associate*.

Production: Mary Beth Trimper, *Production Director*. Evi Seoud, *Assistant Production*

Manager. Cindy Range, *Production Assistant*.

Graphic Services: Randy Bassett, *Image Database Supervisor*. Robert Duncan and Michael Logusz, *Imaging Specialists*. Pamela A. Reed, *Photography Coordinator*. Gary Leach, *Macintosh Artist*.

Product Design: Cynthia Baldwin, *Product Design Manager*. Cover Design: Michelle DiMercurio, *Art Director*. Page Design: Pamela A. E. Galbreath, *Senior Art Director*.

Copyright Notice

of this work have added value to the underlying factual material herein through one or more of the following: unique and original selection, coordination, expression, arrangement, and classification of the information. All rights to this publication will be vigorously defended.

The Grapes of Wrath

John Steinbeck

1939

Introduction

When *The Grapes of Wrath* was published on March 14, 1939, it created a national sensation for its depiction of the devastating effects of the Great Depression of the 1930s. By the end of April, it was selling 2,500 copies a day—a remarkable number considering the hard economic times. In May, the novel was a number-one best-seller, selling at a rate of 10,000 copies a week. By the end of 1939, close to a half million copies had been sold.

John Steinbeck was shocked by the

tremendous response to his novel. Almost overnight, he was transformed from a respected, struggling writer into a public sensation. Yet *The Grapes of Wrath* was bound to cause controversy in a country experiencing a decade of major social upheaval during the Depression. With the novel's publication, Steinbeck found himself immersed in a great national debate over the migrant labor problem. Many people were shocked by the poverty and hopelessness of the story, and others denied that such circumstances could happen in America. Admidst the controversy, people who had never read a book before bought a copy of *The Grapes of Wrath*. At $2.75 per copy, it was affordable and quickly sold out. Libraries had waiting lists for the novel that were months long.

It was perhaps inevitable that such an epic novel would cause a sensation. With the exception of Margaret Mitchell's *Gone with the Wind* (1936), *The Grapes of Wrath* was the publishing event of the decade. Widespread charges of obscenity were brought against the novel, and it was banned and burned in Buffalo, New York; East Saint Louis, Illinois; and Kern County, California, where much of the novel is set. In fact, the novel remains one of the most frequently banned books in the United States, according to school and library associations. The book was denounced in Congress by Representative Lyle Boren of Oklahoma, who called the novel's depiction of migrant living conditions a vulgar lie. Charges were made that "obscenity" had been included in the book in large part to sell more copies. Eventually, First Lady

Eleanor Roosevelt stepped in to praise the book and defend Steinbeck against his critics. In 1940, the novel won the Pulitzer Prize. Yet, at the time, such were the pressures of Steinbeck's celebrity that he described fame as "a pain in the ass."

The popularity of the novel has endured. It is estimated that it has sold fifteen million copies since its publication. For almost sixty years, Steinbeck's novel has been a classic in American literature; it has been translated into several languages, including French, German, and Japanese. *The Grapes of Wrath* has also been an integral part of the school curriculum in America since the end of World War II.

Author Biography

John Ernst Steinbeck was born on February 27, 1902, in Salinas, California. He was the third of four children, and the only son born to John Ernst Sr. and Olive Hamilton Steinbeck. A fourth child, Mary, was born in 1909. Olive Steinbeck had been a teacher in one-room schools in Big Sur, California, before her marriage to John Sr. After their marriage, the Steinbecks moved to Salinas in 1894, where John Sr. became a manager at the Sperry Flour Mill and later served as treasurer of Monterey County.

Salinas is located one hundred miles south of San Francisco, near Monterey Bay. At the time of Steinbeck's birth, it was a town with a population of approximately three thousand. During John's early childhood, the first automobiles could be seen rumbling through town. Family life was apparently secure and happy. Steinbeck's father quickly recognized his son's talents and eventually both parents encouraged Steinbeck in his dream to become a writer.

Steinbeck's best-known works of fiction, including *The Grapes of Wrath* and *Of Mice and Men* (1937), are set in central California, where he grew up. In particular, one of the principal locales in *The Grapes of Wrath* is the San Joaquin Valley, a fertile farming area which lies east of the Gabilan Mountains. Although Steinbeck's family was solidly middle class, he had to earn his own money during high school. He worked on nearby ranches during the summer and he also delivered newspapers on his bike, exploring Salinas's Mexican neighborhood and Chinatown. Later, he would use his boyhood memories of these places in his stories and novels.

As a child, Steinbeck was shy and often a loner. Other children teased him about his large ears, and he responded by withdrawing into books. He was an excellent storyteller, a lifelong trait that found its natural outlet in his writing. In 1915, Steinbeck entered Salinas High School and began writing stories and sending them anonymously to magazines. He was president of his senior class and graduated in a class of twenty-four students. Steinbeck enrolled in Stanford University in 1919, which he would attend on and off for the next six years. He left Stanford in 1925 without a degree.

During the summers and other times he was away from college, Steinbeck worked as a farm laborer, sometimes living with migrants in the farm's bunkhouse. After leaving school for good in 1925, Steinbeck took a job on a freighter and went to New York City. There he worked in construction and later as a reporter for *The American* for twenty-five dollars a week. But he was fired because his reporting was not "objective" enough. When he failed to find a publisher for his short stories, he returned to California by freighter. In 1930, Steinbeck married Carol Henning and settled in Pacific Grove. While Carol worked at various jobs to support John's career, he continued to write.

Finally, in 1935 his first successful novel, *Tortilla Flat*, was published. In 1937, *Of Mice and Men* became an immediate best-seller, and Steinbeck became a respected writer. He adapted this novel into a play, which won the New York Drama Critics Circle Award in 1937.

The stress that came with success and fame hastened the collapse of Steinbeck's marriage, which ended in 1942. A year later, Steinbeck married dancer-singer Gwen Conger, with whom he had two sons—his only children—before their divorce in 1948. By 1950, Steinbeck had married his third wife, Elaine Scott.

After leaving California in the early 1940s, Steinbeck lived the rest of his life in New York City and on Long Island in New York. His final novel, published the year before he was awarded the Nobel Prize for Literature, was *The Winter of Our Discontent*. The story focuses on the decline of the moral climate in America. When he won the Nobel Prize in 1962, only five other Americans had received the award: Sinclair Lewis, Eugene O'Neill, Pearl Buck, William Faulkner, and Ernest Hemingway.

Accepting the Nobel Prize in Sweden, Steinbeck said: "The ancient commission of the writer has not changed. He is charged with exposing our many grievous faults and failures, with dredging up to the light our dark and dangerous dreams for the purpose of improvement. Furthermore, the writer is delegated to declare and to celebrate man's proven capacity for greatness of heart and spirit—

for gallantry in defeat—for courage, compassion, and love. In the endless war against weakness and despair, these are the bright rally-flags of hope and of emulation. I hold that a writer who does not passionately believe in the perfectibility of man, has no dedication nor any membership in literature."

Steinbeck wrote no fiction after receiving the Nobel Prize. His reporting on the Vietnam War for *Newsday*, a Long Island newspaper, in 1967 caused many people to label him a hawk and a warmonger. Steinbeck died following a heart attack on December 20, 1968. He was sixty-six years old. His ashes were buried in Salinas, California.

Chapters 1-11: Leaving Oklahoma

The Grapes of Wrath follows the trials and tribulations of the Joad family as they leave the dust bowl of Oklahoma for a better life in California. The narrative begins as Tom Joad hitchhikes across the Oklahoma panhandle to his parents' forty-acre farm. Tom has just been paroled after serving four years in prison for manslaughter. He meets ex-preacher Jim Casy, who is alone and singing by the side of the road. Casy recounts his own fall, his doubts about the saving grace of religion, and his growing sense of a collective human spirit. When the two men arrive at the Joad farm, they find it abandoned. A neighbor, Muley Graves, explains how the banks have repossessed the family farms, forcing people to leave. The smell of their dinner brings the sheriff and the men have to hide in the fields.

At the house of Tom's Uncle John, Tom and Casy meet up with the Joads: Granma; Grampa; Ma; Pa; Noah, the eldest son, who is slightly crazy; Al, sixteen, who is a "tomcat" and a mechanic; Rose of Sharon who is four months pregnant and married to Connie Rivers; and Ruthie and Winfield, Tom's younger sister and brother. The Joads have seen handbills announcing work in California and are preparing for their departure by selling their possessions, slaughtering their pigs, and loading a secondhand car. Casy asks to go along and is accepted into the family. When the time comes to leave, Grampa refuses to go. He has lived his whole life in Oklahoma and he can't imagine starting over. At Tom's suggestion, they get him drunk and load him on the truck with the rest of the family.

Chapters 12-21: Into California

Once they leave Oklahoma, Tom becomes a fugitive for breaking the terms of his parole. The Joad family meets the Wilsons, another family traveling west. They camp together, and Grampa dies of a stroke in the Wilsons' tent. The Wilsons and Joads drive west on Route 66 until a rod in the Wilsons' car breaks. Ma refuses to let the families split up, so they wait while the young men search for a wrecking yard and a replacement part. At the California border, the families ready themselves for a night crossing of the Mojave desert. A man and his son, heading east, warn the group about the dire conditions facing migrants in California. Upon crossing the Colorado River into California, things take a turn for the worse. Noah vows to stay and wanders off along the river. The Wilsons decide not to go any farther. As the Joads make their night crossing, Granma dies. Ma, who is lying next to her, refuses to say a word for fear that they will stop.

They leave Granma's body with the local coroner and make their way to a Hooverville, a camp where the migrant workers live. The rumors they have heard are true. There is little or no work. The basic necessities are hard to come by and the residents of the state do not want "Okies" around. A contractor drives up looking for produce pickers. It is a trick—a sheriff's deputy is with the contractor and plans to arrest the "Okies" and clean out the camp. In the ensuing altercation, the deputy is knocked unconscious by Tom. Casy takes the blame and tells Tom to escape so he won't be returned to Oklahoma. Upon hearing about Casy's sacrifice, Uncle John gets drunk to drown his feeling of worthlessness. The family hears a rumor that the Hooverville will be burned to the ground by townspeople who are angry at the migrants. Tom leaves a message at the store for Connie, who has suddenly disappeared, abandoning Rose of Sharon for dreams of a three-dollar-a-day job driving corporate tractors in Oklahoma. As they leave, an angry mob warns them not to return. Tom drives the truck south in search of the government camp, with the glow of the Hooverville burning in the night behind them.

Chapters 22-30: The Reality of California

The Joads are lucky to arrive at the government camp just as a site has opened up. In the morning, neighbors share their breakfast with Tom and together they go to work for a small grower who is forced by the Farmers Association and Bank of the West to offer low wages. The grower warns them about a plot to shut down the government camp that Saturday night. Ma enjoys a tour of the facilities given by the camp's governing committee. Rose of Sharon, abandoned and vulnerable, has two frightening encounters with an evangelist. Pa, John, and Al search for work without luck.

That Saturday night, three outsiders try to start a fight at the dance but their attempt is quickly thwarted. At the same moment, the deputies try to enter the camp under the pretext of restoring law and order. They, too, are turned back.

Although the conditions in the government camp are the best the Joads have encountered, they cannot find work. They pack the car and drive north. A man tells them about work picking peaches. When they arrive, they are escorted by the police into the orchard. They soon realize they have been brought in as strikebreakers. That night, Tom slips under the fence surrounding the orchard and discovers Casy leading the strike. They are ambushed by an agent of the growers and Casy is killed. Tom avenges his friend by killing the agent. He sneaks back to camp and has to hide since the cut on his face will give him away.

With Casy's death, the strike is broken and the pickers' pay is cut in half. The Joads drive north, eventually commandeering half of an abandoned boxcar. Tom hides in the marsh. Ruthie gets in a fight and boasts that her brother has killed two men. Ma goes to the marsh to send her son away. When she expresses her concern for his safety, he soothes her with what he has learned from Casy.

The next day, a torrential rain falls and flood-waters rise. Rose of Sharon's sudden labor prevents the Joads from leaving the boxcar for higher ground. Several families stay to help Pa dig a dike. A giant tree topples, spins slowly through the water, and destroys the dike. The waters quickly rise, eliminating any chance for immediate escape. Rose of Sharon delivers a stillborn child. Eventually, the family is able to leave the boxcar. Al stays behind with his new bride-to-be. The family wades through the flood until they find a barn on higher ground. Inside are a boy and his father who is near death. As they settle in, Ma and Rose of Sharon exchange a look, and the novel ends with Rose of Sharon suckling the starving man with her breast milk.

Inserted into this narrative are sixteen chapters of varying prose styles and subjects. Although they do not directly involve members of the Joad family, these chapters introduce topics that are thematically or symbolically relevant to the main narrative. The first and last interchapters, for example, address the weather and climate: the first announcing the dust and its impact on the land, the last speaking to the California rain and floods. The second interchapter follows a turtle as it patiently makes its way over the land. Other chapters critique ownership, capitalism, and consumerism, or address the social impact of technology, cars and tractors. One provides a history of California that highlights how settlers stole the land from the Mexicans. Another explores how the Oklahomans killed the Indians for their land. Several interchapters follow the great westward movement of 200,000 people over Route 66 and chart their social evolution from farmers to migrants and their new relationships to canneries, land owners, and banks.

Characters

Jim Casy

Jim Casy accompanies the Joad family on their journey from Oklahoma to California. He is a former preacher who has given up both Christian fundamentalism and sexuality, and is ready for a new life dedicated to helping people like the Joads. He is honest, compassionate, and courageous. Casy's new "religion" is based on love and a belief in each person's soul as well as an all-inclusive soul, the "Holy Spirit" of humanity. As critics have noted, these non-secular views of humanity can be traced to the transcendentalist philosophy of Walt Whitman and Ralph Waldo Emerson. Casy is a new convert to this transcendentalism.

Casy's initials (J. C.) have been cited as evidence that his character is a symbol of Jesus Christ. Moreover, his words and actions in the novel parallel those of Jesus Christ. For instance, he takes the blame for the deputy's beating at the Hooverville, and is taken to jail instead of Tom. His selfless struggle eventually leads him to become a strike organizer and leader. He is killed for this activism, and his last words recall those of Christ on the cross: "You fellas don' know what you're doin'." Through his actions, he helps Tom Joad to choose the same selfless path. Casy's new personal identity is an expression of a larger self, although such self-realization earns society's disapproval and is responsible for his murder.

Muley Graves

Muley Graves is a classic example of the stubborn man; even his name is a pun on this trait. At the beginning of the novel, he refuses to leave Oklahoma. He is homeless and his isolation drives him somewhat insane. His pessimism and blind violence against "the Bank" and its representatives are rejected by the stronger Joads, whose essential optimism infuses their journey to California.

Al Joad

Al Joad is the third Joad son; he is younger than Noah and Tom, to whom he looks for guidance. Al is fond of cars and girls. He assumes a greater position in the family because of his mechanical knowledge, but he is not always mature enough to deal with the responsibility. He helps drive the family to California. He wants to leave the family and go on his own, but duty and love force him to stay.

Grampa Joad

Grampa Joad is rowdy and vigorous, like a "frantic child." He refuses to leave the family's farm in Oklahoma and has to be drugged so that the family can begin their journey. But Grampa's vigor declines drastically when he leaves the land he has grown up on, and he dies on the first night of the trip. Both Granma and Grampa die because they are incapable of absorbing a new, difficult experience. In addition, Grampa's stroke is probably caused in part by the "medicine" that Ma and Tom give him.

Granma Joad

Granma Joad is deeply religious and energetic; she has thrived in her war of words with Grampa because "she was as mean as her husband." She is unable to adapt to a new way of life and the loss of her husband. She dies as the family crosses the Mojave Desert, and her burial in a pauper's grave violates her wishes. Her death outweighs the achievement of finally reaching California and foreshadows the reality to come.

Ma Joad

Ma Joad is the matriarch and foundation of the Joad family. She is the basis for the family's strength in the face of all their hardships. Ma Joad often behaves heroically for the sake of the family, yet she also expresses her fears. Nonetheless, Ma is brave and intelligent. She is an example of the indestructible woman who at times is ignorant, wary, and suspicious of strangers. She has much family pride and is active and assertive on their behalf.

Ma Joad displays numerous traditionally masculine qualities without losing her femininity or her maternal instinct. She assumes authority to prevent the weakening of the family unit. Once Ma Joad assumes the power as the head of the family, the others do not resist her. She passes her strength and wisdom on to her daughter, Rose of Sharon. Ma's transformation is seen when she finally comes to accept commitments to people beyond her family. As she tells the Hooper store clerk, "I'm learnin' one thing good…. If you're in trouble or hurt or need—go to poor people. They're the only ones that'll help—the only ones."

Noah Joad

Noah is the eldest Joad child. Slow, deliberate, and never angry, he is often mistaken as mentally challenged. Pa treats him kindly, because of his guilt over Noah's birth; scared by Ma's struggles, Pa tried to help deliver Noah and injured his head. Midway through the journey to California, Noah gives up the struggle to survive the arduous trip.

Pa Joad

Before the Joad family leaves Oklahoma, Pa Joad is considered the head of the clan. As the family travels, however, Pa loses his authority in the family to Ma Joad and his son Al. Ma's enduring faith in the family eventually gives her final say on decisions, while Al's mechanical ability makes him important because the family needs the car for their journey to California. This loss of Pa Joad's authority represents the shift in values within the family. Pa carries the family's burdens, although he is constantly challenged by Ma. Each time Ma asserts her newfound leadership, she meets with Pa's resentment. Nevertheless, he realizes that she has necessarily usurped his authority and does not act out his anger. His powerlessness is somewhat exorcised when he leads the boxcar migrants in a group effort to save their temporary homes from the flood. Throughout the novel, Pa's common sense, dependability, and steadfastness contrast with Uncle John's melancholy and Connie's immaturity.

Ruthie Joad

Twelve years old, Ruthie is the youngest daughter of the Joads. She is a selfish individual who has not learned her correct place in the social group. She learns a hard lesson when she is ostracized by the other children at the government camp for trying to take over their croquet game. In a childish fight, she reveals to another child that Tom has killed a man. This disclosure finally forces Tom to flee the family. Ruthie has a tendency towards cruelty that is aggravated by the family's hard luck. Her childish behavior shows how poverty can make even an innocent person harsh.

Tom Joad

Tom Joad killed a man in self-defense and has just been released from an Oklahoma state prison. Tom is depicted as wary, insensitive, skeptical, matter-of-fact, and confident. He has an ability to adapt and is a shrewd judge of character. At the beginning of the novel, Tom is only concerned with survival and keeping his prison record a secret. He is looking for peace and quiet at his family's farm. He undergoes a transformation in the course of the novel; by the end of the story, he believes in the potential of humanity's perfection and universality of spirit. Tom demonstrates this through social action, for instance, as he organizes the migrant farm laborers in California. Although Tom is emotionally numb from his experience in prison, he is by nature inquisitive: he always asks questions and is always seeking answers in life. Tom is forced to leave his family at the end of the novel.

Tom Joad Sr.

See Pa Joad

Uncle John Joad

John Joad, or Uncle John, is a prisoner of his guilt over his wife's death years before. Uncle John's melancholy balances the family's experiences. His sense of guilt causes him to blame all the family's misfortunes on what he thinks of as his sin: his failure to call a doctor when his wife complained of illness. As a result of this emotional scar, he has become an alcoholic. Uncle John's lifelong sense of guilt is transformed into anger when he sets Rose of Sharon's stillborn baby afloat in a box on the river to remind townspeople that they are starving children by their failure to help the migrants.

William James Joad

See Grampa Joad

Winfield Joad

Ten-year-old Winfield is the youngest child of the Joad family. He is treated cruelly by his sister Ruthie, yet Winfield retains his innocence. Unlike their grandparents, who die when uprooted from Oklahoma, the youngest Joads are "planted" in California and will perhaps take root there, fulfilling Ma's statement that "the people will go on."

Floyd Knowles

When the Joad family meets him outside of Bakersfield, Floyd Knowles tries to warn Al and the other men about the difficulties they will face in California. After Al helps him fix his car, he tells the family of potential work. When a contractor comes to the Hooverville to look for workers, Floyd's questions lead the police to try to arrest him. During the scuffle, Jim Casy kicks the deputy in the head and takes the blame for the fight.

Jim Rawley

A small, friendly man, Jim Rawley is the manager of the government camp. He makes Ma feel comfortable her first day at the camp, and his simple kindness almost drives Ma to tears. Even though Pa mistrusts him at first, to Ma he symbolizes the goodness of a community who allows the poor their dignity.

Media Adaptations

- *The Grapes of Wrath* was adapted as a film by Twentieth Century Fox in 1940. The film was directed by John Ford and starred Henry Fonda as Tom Joad; Jane Darwell as Ma Joad; Doris Bowdon as Rose of Sharon; and John Carradine as Jim Casy. The screenplay was written by Nunnally Johnson; the cinematography was by Gregg Toland. The film won two Academy Awards: for Best Director (John Ford) and Best Supporting Actress (Jane Darwell). It also won two awards from the New York Film Critics Circle for 1940: Best Director (Ford), and Best Film. Available from Fox Video, Baker & Taylor Video, Home Vision Cinema.

- *The Grapes of Wrath* was also adapted as an audio cassette (58 minutes), Dolby processed, published by Harper Audio in New York City. Read by Henry Fonda, who starred as Tom Joad in the 1940 movie, the sound recording contains excerpts from the novel about the plight of the migrants during the 1930s. Harper Audio, 1994.

- The novel was also adapted as a 58-minute audio cassette by Caedmon Inc. in 1978.

Connie Rivers

Connie is Rose of Sharon's nineteen-year-old husband who is "frightened and bewildered" by the changes his wife's pregnancy has brought upon her. He constantly talks of educating himself by correspondence in order to get a good job, but he is all talk and no action. He often tells Rose of Sharon that he should have stayed behind in Oklahoma and taken a job driving a tractor. Although he is described as "a good hard worker [who] would make a good husband," he eventually deserts Rose of Sharon because he has no faith in the family's struggle to find a better life in California. Connie's values can be connected with those of "the Bank": a focus on acquiring money and learning about technology in order to advance in the world. He also serves as a contrast and warning to Al Joad, whose fondness for the ladies could put him in the same situation. Unlike Connie, Al sticks it out with his family and wife.

Rose of Sharon Joad Rivers

Rose of Sharon is the elder Joad daughter. Still a teen, she is already married and pregnant. Throughout most of the novel, she thinks only of herself and her unborn child. She is depicted as a sheltered and thoughtless teenager. Yet Rose of Sharon undergoes a transformation during her pregnancy, which coincides with the difficult journey to California.

With Ma's guidance, she grows from child to adult. As she prepares to change roles from daughter to mother, she becomes "balanced, careful, wise." She endures much hardship, including the birth of her stillborn child, and by the end of the novel, she is ready to take her place with Ma Joad as a pillar of the family. It is clear that Rose of Sharon will succeed Ma as matriarch; in fact, she becomes something of an extension of Ma. Right until the end of the novel, she is referred to as a girl, but in the final scene, Steinbeck makes clear that Rose of Sharon and Ma are equals. He writes, "and the two women looked deep into each other." When Rose of Sharon feeds the starving man from her breast, she takes her place as the indestructible matriarch who, by her selfless act, comes to signify hope and survival of the people. It is through Rose of Sharon's selfless human gesture that the author symbolizes and emphasizes the most effective method of survival against oppression and exploitation: that people must develop compassion for their fellow human beings.

Rosasharn Joad Rivers

See Rose of Sharon Joad Rivers

Ivy and Sairy Wilson

Ivy and Sairy Wilson are a married couple that the Joads meet on the first night of their journey. They camp next to the Joads, and lend their tent to the sick Grampa, who subsequently dies. The Wilsons split from the Joads at California's Mojave Desert because Sairy Wilson is dying and is in too much pain to continue. That action contrasts with the Joads' choice, which is to turn back in spite of death.

Themes

Hope

The Joads experience many hardships, deprivations, and deaths, and at the end of the novel are barely surviving. Nevertheless, the mood of the novel is optimistic. This positive feeling is derived from the growth of the Joad family as they begin to realize a larger group consciousness at the end of the novel. The development of this theme can be seen particularly in Ma Joad, from her focus on keeping the family together to her recognition of the necessity of identifying with the group. "Use' ta be the fambly was fust. It ain't so now. It's anybody. Worse off we get, the more we got to do," Ma says in the final chapter.

Hope comes from the journey that educates and enlightens some of the Joads, including Ma, Tom, Pa, John, Rose of Sharon, and also Jim Casy. On the surface, the family's long journey is an attempt at the "good life," the American dream. Yet this is not the only motive. In fact, the members of the family who cannot see beyond this materialistic goal leave the family along the way: Noah, Connie, and Al. The Joads travel from their traditional life that offered security, through chaos on the road and on into California. There, they look for a new way of life, and a larger understanding of the world. And whether or not the remaining Joads live or die in

California, their journey has been successful. Hope survives, as the people survive, because they want to understand and master their lives in the face of continual discouragement.

Class Conflict

The conflict in the novel between the impoverished migrants and the established, secure business people and Californians serves as a strong criticism of economic injustice. In fact, *The Grapes of Wrath* can be read as a social comment on the economic disasters of the time. The migrants' agrarian way of life has all but disappeared, threatened not only by nature's drought and dust storms, but also by big farms and financial establishments, called "the Bank." At the beginning of the novel, the owners and the banks push the tenants off of their land. Later the arrival of hundreds of thousands of poor people causes conflict in California.

The migrants represent trouble for businessmen in the form of higher taxes, labor unions, and possible government interference. The potential for future conflict is understood by all the business owners: if the migrants ever organize, they will seriously threaten the financial establishment. The Joads' travails dramatize such economic and social conflicts. In California, the conflict between the two sides grows violent as the migrants' desperation increases. The government camps are harassed or even burned down by angry state residents with financial interests.

There are also conflicts within the family that reflect the materialistic concerns of this class conflict. Rose of Sharon is preoccupied with her pregnancy and daydreams of the future. Her husband, Connie, wanted to stay in Oklahoma, and he does little to help the family on the road. Finally he disappears. Uncle John is consumed with worry and frustration. The children, Ruthie and Winfield, are selfish and restless. The hardships of dispossessed families are made personal and individual in the account of the Joads.

Fanaticism

Fanaticism—both as a religious fundamentalism and as a social phenomenon—is condemned in the novel. During Tom's first meeting with Jim Casy, the former preacher talks about his discovery that organized religion denies life, particularly sexuality. He in fact had found a connection between the "Holy Spirit" and sexuality when he was a preacher. Later, in the government camp, Rose of Sharon is frightened by a fanatic religious woman's warning that dancing is sinful and that it means that Rose of Sharon will lose her baby. In addition, the religious fanatic tells Ma that religion approves of an economic class system that incorporates poverty. She tells Ma: "(A preacher) says they's wicketness in that camp. He says, 'The poor is tryin' to be rich.' He says, 'They's dancin' an' huggin' when they should be wailin' an' moanin' in sin.'" This type of religious fanaticism is shown to be a denial of life and is associated with business in its economic deprivation and denial.

One of the most profound lessons from the story of the Joads and their real-life American counterparts is that one of the causes of the crises of the 1930s in California was social fanaticism and prejudice shown to the "Okies." The fear of the migrants, combined with the lack of faith in the government's ability to solve the temporary problems, often caused violence. It also led to such shameful events as starvation, malnutrition, and homelessness. In retrospect, it is obvious that World War II "solved" the migrant problem by absorbing the manpower into the war effort. How much better it would have been if California had developed emergency solutions for this period of great social transition that could have served as an historical example.

Topics for Further Study

- Compare and contrast the current conditions of migrant farm workers in California with those of the migrants of the 1930s. Research current labor laws protecting the rights of these workers today. Have conditions improved in the last sixty years?

- Besides drought, one cause for the tragedy of the Dust Bowl was poor farming practices—including overgrazing by cattle and failure of farmers to rotate their crops—which exhausted the land's resources. How have farming practices changed since the 1930s to protect and manage the land to help ensure it will remain fertile for future generations?

- The mass migration of the Okies to California was caused by drought and economic depression. What other important mass migrations have occurred in U. S. history? Research the reasons behind these migrations and discuss the effects they have had on local economies and societies.

Individual vs. Society

The novel demonstrates the individual's instinct to organize communities within the groups of migrants in roadside camps. "In the evening a strange thing happened: the twenty families became one family, the children were the children of all. The loss of home became one loss, and the golden time in the West was one dream." The people cooperate because it is beneficial to their welfare in order to survive. Yet Steinbeck develops the concept of the group beyond the political, social, and moral level to include the mystical and transcendental. Jim Casy reflects this when he says: "Maybe all men got one big soul everybody's a part of." The conversion of Tom, Ma, Rose of Sharon, and Casy to a "we" state of mind occurs over the course of the novel. As they gradually undergo suffering, they learn to transcend their own pain and individual needs. At the end, all four are able to recognize the nature and needs of others. The process of transcendence that occurs in these characters illustrates Steinbeck's belief in the capacity of humanity to move from what he calls an "I" to a "We" consciousness.

The Joads are also on an inward journey. For them, suffering and homelessness become the means for spiritual growth and a new consciousness. Ma sums up this new consciousness and what it means to her when she says: "Use' ta be the fambly was fust. It ain't so now. It's anybody." Yet although each of the four characters undergoes a spiritual transformation, each also finds an individual way to help others in the world and to take action. At the end, Tom has decided to become a leader in the militant organizing of the migrants. Ma accepts her commitments to people other than her family. Rose of Sharon loses her baby but comes to understand the "we" of the starving man to whom she blissfully gives life as if he were her child. Casy, who has been jailed, reappears as a strike leader and union organizer, having discovered that he must work to translate his understanding of the holiness of life into social action. Casy dies when vigilantes attack the strikers and kill him first.

Steinbeck makes clear that this potential for transcendental consciousness is what makes human beings different from other creatures in nature. In Chapter 14, Steinbeck describes humanity's willingness to "die for a concept" as the "one quality [that] is the foundation of Manself, and this one quality is man, distinctive in the universe."

Commitment

Steinbeck develops extensively the theme of social commitment. Both Casy and Tom were inspired to make Christ-like sacrifices. When Jim Casy surrenders to the deputies in place of Tom and Floyd, Jim is acting on his commitment to love all people. He later becomes a labor organizer and dies in his efforts. His statement to Tom, "An' sometimes I love 'em fit to bust…," exemplifies his commitment. In Tom, the development of commitment is even more striking. At the beginning of the novel, Tom is determined to avoid involvement with people. After his experiences on the journey and through his friendship with Casy, Tom becomes committed to social justice. His commitment extends to a mystical identification with the people. When Ma worries that Tom may also be killed like Casy, Tom tells her: "Then I'll be ever'where—wherever you look. Wherever there's a fight so hungry people can eat, I'll be there. Wherever they's a cop beatin' up a guy, I'll be there. If Casy knowed, why, I'll be in the way guys yell when they're mad an' I'll be in the way kids laugh when they're hungry an' they know supper's ready. An' when our folks eat the stuff they raise an' live in the houses they build—why I'll be there."

Style

Point of View

The novel is narrated in the third-person voice ("he"/"she"/"it"). What is particularly significant about this technique is that the point of view varies in tone and method, depending on the author's purpose. The novel's distinctive feature is its sixteen inserted, or intercalary, chapters (usually the odd-numbered chapters) that provide documentary information for the reader. These chapters give social and historical background of the mid-1930s Depression era, especially as it affects migrants like the Joads.

These inserted chapters range from descriptions of the Dust Bowl and agricultural conditions in Oklahoma, to California's history, to descriptions of roads leading west from Oklahoma. In the more restricted chapters that focus on the Joads, the point of view shifts to become close and dramatic. In addition, many of the inserted chapters contain basic symbols of the novel: land, family, and the conflict between the migrants and the people who represent the bank and agribusiness. The turtle in Chapter 3 symbolizes Nature's struggle and the will to survive. It characterizes the will to survive of the Joads and "the people."

Setting

John Steinbeck wrote some of his best fiction about the area where he grew up. The territory that Steinbeck wrote about is an area covering thousands of square miles in central California. He particularly used the Long Valley as a setting in his fiction, which extends south of Salinas, Steinbeck's hometown. The Long Valley, covering more than one hundred miles, lies between the Gabilan Mountains to the east and the Santa Lucia Mountains on the Pacific Coast. The major site of *The Grapes of Wrath* is the San Joaquin Valley, which lies east of the Long Valley and the Gabilan Mountains. The Long Valley is also the general setting for *Of Mice and Men* (1937) and *East of Eden* (1952), two of Steinbeck's other well-known works. This rich agricultural area is an ironic setting for a novel that examines the economic and social problems affecting people during the Depression. It was no promised land for the Joads and others like them.

One of Steinbeck's major achievements is his remarkable descriptions of the environment and nature's effects on social history. He was also ahead of his time in writing about the circumstances of the migrant workers and small farmers fighting corporate farms and the financial establishment decades before such subjects gained national press coverage in the 1970s.

Symbolism

The major symbol in the novel is the family,

which stands for the larger "family" of humanity. The Joads are at the center of the dramatic aspects of the novel, and they illustrate human strengths and weaknesses. Dangers in nature and in society disrupt the family, but they survive economic and natural disasters, just as humanity does. At the end, the Joads themselves recognize they are part of a larger family. The land itself is a symbol that is equated in the novel with a sense of personal identity. What the Joads actually suffer when they lose their Oklahoma farm is a sense of identity, which they struggle to rediscover during their journey and in California. Pa Joad, especially, loses his spirit after the family is "tractored off" their land. He must cede authority in the family to Ma after their loss.

There is also a sequence of Judeo-Christian symbols throughout the novel. The Joads, like the Israelites, are a homeless and persecuted people looking for the promised land. Jim Casy can be viewed as a symbol of Jesus Christ, who began His mission after a period of solitude in the wilderness. Casy is introduced in the novel after a similar period of retreat. And later, when Casy and Tom meet in the strikers' tent, Casy says he has "been a-gin' into the wilderness like Jesus to try to find out sumpin." Also, Jim Casy has the same initials as Jesus Christ. Like Christ, Casy finally offers himself as the sacrifice to save his people. Casy's last words to the man who murders him are significant: "Listen, you fellas don' know what you're doing." And just before he dies, Casy repeats: "You don' know what you're a-doin'." When Jesus Christ was crucified,

He said, "Father forgive them; they know not what they do." Tom becomes Casy's disciple after his death. Tom is ready to continue his teacher's work, and it has been noted that two of Jesus's disciples were named Thomas.

Biblical symbols from both Old and New Testament stories occur throughout the novel. Twelve Joads start on their journey from Oklahoma, corresponding to the twelve tribes of Israel or the twelve disciples of Christ (with Jim Casy, the Christ figure) on their way to spiritual enlightenment by a messiah. Like Lot's wife, Grampa is reluctant to leave his homeland, and his refusal to let go of the past brings his death. Later, the narrative emphasizes this symbolism when Tom selects a Scripture verse for Grampa's burial that quotes Lot. The shifts between the Old and New testaments coalesce with Jim Casy, whose ideas about humanity and a new social gospel parallel Christ's new religion two thousand years ago. Biblical myths also inform the final scene through a collection of symbols that demonstrate the existence of a new order in the Joads' world. As the Joads seek refuge from the flood in a dry barn, the narrative offers symbols of the Old Testament deluge (Noah's ark), the New Testament stable where Christ was born (the barn), and the mysterious rite of Communion as Rose of Sharon breast feeds the starving man. With this ending, it is clear that this is a new beginning for the Joads. All the symbols express hope and regeneration despite the continuing desperate circumstances.

Allusion

Allusions, or literary references, to grapes and vineyards are made throughout the novel, carrying Biblical and economic connotations. The title of the novel, from Julia Ward Howe's poem "The Battle Hymn of the Republic," is itself an allusion dating back to the Bible's Old Testament. In Isaiah 63:4-6, a man tramples grapes in his wrath: "For the day of vengeance was in my heart, and the year for my redeeming work had come. I looked, but there was no helper; I stared, but there was no one to sustain me; so my own arm brought me victory, and my wrath sustained me. I trampled down peoples in my anger, I crushed them in my wrath, and I poured out their lifeblood on the earth." Steinbeck's first wife, Carol, suggested the title after hearing the lyrics of the patriotic hymn: "Mine eyes have seen the glory of the coming of the Lord / He is trampling out the vintage where the grapes of wrath are stored." Steinbeck loved the title and wrote to his agent: "I think it is Carol's best title so far. I like it because it is a march and this book is a kind of march— because it is in our own revolutionary tradition and because in reference to this book it has a large meaning. And I like it because people know the 'Battle Hymn' who don't know the 'Star Spangled Banner.'"

Indeed, Steinbeck knew that his unfinished novel was revolutionary and that it would be condemned by many people as Communist propaganda. So the title was especially suitable because it carried an American patriotic stamp that

Steinbeck hoped would deflect charges of leftist influence. He decided that he wanted the complete hymn, its words and music, printed on the endpapers at the front and back of the book. He wrote his publisher: "The fascist crowd will try to sabotage this book because it is revolutionary. They will try to give it the communist angle. However, the 'Battle Hymn' is American and intensely so. Further, every American child learns it and then forgets the words. So if both the words and music are there the book is keyed into the American scene from the beginning."

Allegory

An allegory is a story in which characters and events have a symbolic meaning that points to general human truths. The turtle in Chapter 3 is the novel's best-known use of allegory. The patient turtle proceeds along a difficult journey over the dust fields of Oklahoma, often meeting obstacles, but always able to survive. Like the Joads, the turtle is moving southwest, away from the drought. When a trucker swerves to hit the turtle, the creature survives, just as the Joads survive the displacement from their land. Later, Tom finds a turtle and Casy comments: "Nobody can't keep a turtle though. They work at it and work at it, and at last one day they get out and away they go—off somewheres." The turtle is hit by a truck, carried off by Tom, attacked by a cat and a red ant, yet, like the Joads and "the people," he is indomitable with a fierce will to survive. He drags himself through the dust and unknowingly plants a seed for the future.

Troubles for Farmers

The story of the Joads in *The Grapes of Wrath* begins during the Great Depression, but troubles for American farmers had begun years before that. Having enjoyed high crop prices during World War I when supplies of food were short and European markets were disabled, American farmers borrowed heavily from banks to invest in land and equipment. After the war, however, prices for wheat, corn, and other crops plummeted as European farmers returned to their businesses, and American farmers were unable to repay their loans. Thus, in the 1920s, while much of the country was enjoying economic good times, farmers in the United States were in trouble. Banks began to foreclose on loans, often evicting families from their homes. Families who rented acreage from landowners who had defaulted on loans would, like the Joads, be evicted from their homes. The situation, of course, became much worse after the stock market crash of 1929.

The Great Depression and the Dust Bowl

In October, 1929, stock prices dropped precipitously, causing businesses and banks to fail internationally and wiping out the savings of many families. Over the next few years, unemployment rates soared up to twenty-five percent. Although there is much disagreement today about the causes of the stock market crash, many analysts feel that the root of the problem was weaknesses in the coal, textile, and farming industries. Forty percent of the working population in America at the time were farmers. When low crop prices made it difficult or impossible for consumers to buy items such as radios and refrigerators, it had a significant impact on the economy. Goods began to pile up in warehouses with no customers to buy them, leading to the sudden devaluation of company stocks.

The resulting pressure on banks to collect on loans caused them to evict many farmers. However, this wasn't the only problem that plagued farm families. Six years of severe droughts hit the Midwest during the 1930s, causing crops to fail. This, compounded by poor farming practices such as overgrazing and failure to rotate crops, caused the land to wither and dry up. Great dust storms resulted that buried entire communities in sand. More than five million square miles of land from Texas to North Dakota and Arkansas to New Mexico were affected. The Midwest came to be called the Dust Bowl. Although no one escaped the economic pain this caused, small farm families similar to the Joads were the hardest hit. Of these states, Oklahoma was especially hard-pressed. Dispossessed farming families migrated from their state to California by the thousands. These people were called "Okies," although many of the migrant workers were from states other than Oklahoma.

Migrant Camps and Labor Unions

Upon taking office in 1933, President Franklin D. Roosevelt launched a comprehensive agenda of government programs to combat the Depression. Collectively called the New Deal, these programs included new federal agencies designed to create employment opportunities and to improve the lot of workers and the unemployed. Among the many such agencies, the one that most directly touched the Okies' lives was the Farm Security Administration (FSA). Operating under the authority of the Department of Agriculture, in 1936 the FSA began building camps in California in which the homeless migrants could live. Ten such camps were finished by the following year. Steinbeck visited several in his research for *The Grapes of Wrath*. He had the Joads stay at one—the Arvin Sanitary Camp, also called the Weedpatch Camp, in Kern County. The intention was that the orchard owners would follow this example and build larger, better shelters for their migrant workers. This never came about, however, and many families ended up staying at the uncomfortable federal camps for years.

In an attempt to defend their right to earn living wages, migrant workers tried to organize labor unions. Naturally, this was strongly discouraged by the growers, who had the support of the police, who often used brute force. In Kern County in 1938, for example, a mob led by a local sheriff burned down an Okie camp that had become a center for union activity.

Critical Overview

When the novel was published on March 14, 1939, 50,000 copies were on order, a remarkable number for a Depression-era book. By the end of April, *The Grapes of Wrath* was selling 2,500 copies a day. By May, it was the number-one bestseller and was selling 10,000 copies a week. At the end of the year, close to a half-million copies had been sold. It was the top seller of 1939 and remained a bestseller throughout 1940. Since then, the novel has been continuously in print.

Despite its overwhelming popularity, the novel did not receive only favorable reviews. Journalists who wrote early reviews in the newspapers were not particularly impressed with the book. Steinbeck had broken many of the "rules" of fiction writing with his novel. Several reviewers could not understand the novel's unconventional structure. In *Newsweek*, Burton Roscoe wrote that the book has some "magnificent passages" but that it also contains factual errors (including statements that the Dust Bowl extended into eastern Oklahoma when that region of the state had actually remained fertile) and misleading propaganda. A reviewer in *Time* magazine criticized the chapters that did not describe the Joads' story, saying they were "not a successful fiction experiment." In the *New Yorker*, Clifton Fadiman wrote that the novel "dramatizes so that you cannot forget the terrible facts of a wholesale injustice committed by society," yet he also wrote that the latter half of the book was "too detailed."

Similarly, other critics found fault with the structure of the novel. Louis Kronenberger in the *Nation* and Malcolm Cowley in the *New Republic* criticized the latter half of the book and particularly the ending. Other magazine reviewers, especially those writing for monthlies and literary quarterlies, did not focus entirely on the sociological aspects of the novel and considered its artistic merit. These reviewers, on the whole, recognized that Steinbeck had written a seminal and innovative novel. The editor of the *Atlantic Monthly*, Edward Weeks, wrote that it was a "novel whose hunger, passion, and poetry are in direct answer to the angry stirring of our conscience these past seven years." Weeks found the novel almost "too literal, too unsparing," yet he could "only hope that the brutality dodgers will take my word for it that it is essentially a healthy and disciplined work of art."

In the *North American Review*, Charles Angoff defended the novel: "With his latest novel, Mr. Steinbeck at once joins the company of Hawthorne, Melville, Crane and Norris, and easily leaps to the forefront of all his contemporaries. The book has all the earmarks of something momentous, monumental, and memorable…. The book has the proper faults: robust looseness and lack of narrative defi-niteness—faults such as can be found in the Bible, *Moby-Dick, Don Quixote*, and *Jude the Obscure*. The greater artists almost never conform to the rules of their art as set down by those who do not practice it."

One early reviewer who summed up the novel's greatness was Joseph Henry Jackson in the *New York Herald Tribune Books*. Jackson was the book editor of the *San Francisco Chronicle* and had followed Steinbeck's career. He wrote in his review of April 16, 1939, that the novel was the finest book that Steinbeck had written. The review stated: "It is easy to grow lyrical about *The Grapes of Wrath*, to become excited about it, to be stirred to the shouting point by it. Perhaps it is too easy to lose balance in the face of such an extraordinarily moving performance. But it is also true that the effect of the book lasts. The author's employment, for example, of occasional chapters in which the undercurrent of the book is announced, spoken as a running accompaniment to the story, with something of the effect of the sound track in Pare Lorentz's *The River* —that lasts also, stays with you, beats rhythmically in your mind long after you have put the book down. No, the reader's instant response is more than quick enthusiasm, more than surface emotionalism. This novel of America's new disinherited is a magnificent book. It is, I think for the first time, the whole Steinbeck, the mature novelist saying something he must say and doing it with the sure touch of the great artist."

Sources

Charles Angoff, review of *The Grapes of Wrath*, in *North American Review*, Summer, 1939, p. 387.

Malcolm Cowley, review of *The Grapes of Wrath*, in *New Republic*, May 3, 1939, p. 382.

Clifton Fadiman, review of *The Grapes of Wrath*, in *New Yorker*, April 15, 1939, p. 101.

Joseph Henry Jackson, review of *The Grapes of Wrath*, in *New York Herald Tribune Books*, April 16, 1939, p. 3.

Louis Kronenberger, review of *The Grapes of Wrath*, in *Nation*, April 15, 1939.

Burton Roscoe, "Excuse It, Please," *Newsweek*, May 1, 1939, p. 38.

Edward Weeks, review of *The Grapes of Wrath*, in *Atlantic Monthly*, June, 1939.

For Further Study

Frederick I. Carpenter, "The Philosophical Joads," in *College English*, Vol. 2, January, 1941, pp. 324-25.

> Carpenter describes the origins of Steinbeck's social philosophy in American thought from Ralph Waldo Emerson to William James.

Chester E. Eisinger, "Jeffersonian Agrarianism in *The Grapes of Wrath*," in *University of Kansas City Review*, Vol. 14, Winter, 1947, pp. 149-54.

> The critic discusses the relationships between people and the land and how these relationships have changed in the twentieth century.

Joseph Eddy Fontenrose, *John Steinbeck: An Introduction and Interpretation*, Barnes & Noble, 1963.

> The critic discusses the novel's biblical references, its relation to myth, and its stylistic devices.

Warren French, editor, *A Companion to* The Grapes of Wrath, Penguin, 1989.

> A selection of criticism and interpretations of the novel.

Howard Levant, *The Novels of John Steinbeck: A Critical Study*, University of Missouri Press, 1974.

A collection of essays on Steinbeck's novels. Levant examines the role of symbolism and allegory in *The Grapes of Wrath*.

Peter Lisca, *The Wide World of John Steinbeck*, Rutgers University Press, 1958.

Lisca is an important critic of Steinbeck and is knowledgeable about his life and works. His readings of the novel range from Steinbeck's use of symbols and political thought to his work with the migrants.

Paul McCarthy, *John Steinbeck*, Ungar, 1980.

Among other things, the critic discusses Steinbeck's biblical references and the styles of discourse he uses in the novel.

Harry Thornton Moore, *The Novels of John Steinbeck: A First Critical Study*, Kennikat Press, 1968.

Moore discusses how the novel helped the migrant workers and compares this to other works of literature that have had social impact.

Martin Staples Shockly, "The Reception of *The Grapes of Wrath* in Oklahoma," in *American Literature*, Vol. 15, January, 1954, pp. 351-61.

The critic notes how and why the citizens of Oklahoma were offended by the novel.

John Steinbeck, *Working Days: The Journals of "The Grapes of Wrath,"* edited by Robert DeMott, Penguin, 1989.

> Steinbeck's journal entries recording his thoughts and the physical exhaustion he endured while writing his novel.

David Wyatt, *New Essays on "The Grapes of Wrath,"* Cambridge University Press, 1990.

> Wyatt provides an overview of criticism on the novel from 1940–1989.

Lightning Source UK Ltd.
Milton Keynes UK
UKHW020650030822
406784UK00009B/976